THE CHAIRMAN AND
SPEAKER'S ROLE MADE EASY

The Chairman and Speaker's Role Made Easy

Examples of testimonials, installations, fund-raising drives, memorial services, dedications, presentations, patriotic observances and other public ceremonies for organizations, civic groups, churches, schools and other group activities.

by

DAVID BELSON

author of

"What to Say and How to Say It"

and

"Tributes and Forms for Public Occasions."

Printed by Futuro Press, Inc.
476 Broadway, New York 13, N. Y.
200

CONTENTS

INTRODUCTION

The purpose of this book is to make participation in all organizations — civic groups, churches, schools, veterans' and other group activities — easier and more enjoyable. Models and form-books are used by lawyers and the inexperienced participant also should have some pattern to follow. In fulfilling its purpose this book offers no explanations to wade through but illustrates the common situations the user might be called upon to meet. The exemplifications of public ceremonies in this book will afford the user the courage to face a task that is often regarded as an ordeal. Many members and officers of organizations, often without much advance notice, tread a path new to them when they plan or participate in a meeting, a testimonial dinner, a charity drive, memorial service or take part in any one or more of the public events which this work exemplifies. Such participants need the guidance this book offers.

The forms are divided into two sections. Those which concern community, church, school, fraternal, club or other group activities are in Section I. Those of special interest to labor organizations are in Section II.

The names of persons and organizations whenever used in the models are fictitious. Of course, the user must adapt the forms to his special needs as a lawyer would change a form from a form book to fit his client's particular purpose.

It is confidently believed that the use of this book will help group activities to have more productive programs and happier participants — and audiences. It should be useful to program planners, speakers, officers and members of all types of organizations. It is intended as a time-saver for the busy participant in public events and as an aid to those less experienced.

SECTION I

EXAMPLES OF PUBLIC CEREMONIES FOR CIVIC,
FRATERNAL, RELIGIOUS, PATRIOTIC, VETERANS
AND OTHER GROUPS

A. ORGANIZING A CLUB

OPENING

I am happy to be part of the proceedings which will start you on your way to share with others the good things we have discovered for ourselves. Most of the growth of the Speakers' Clubs movement has resulted from this impulse. One who has enjoyed the benefits of membership in a Speakers' Club is eager to pass along the privileges to others. He tells them about it and brings them into his club.

The Speakers' Clubs, International is an organization of men and women interested in personal growth and development through training in speech and leadership. New chapters are welcomed by Speakers' Clubs, International, and new ones are continually being formed extending the benefits of the work to new fields and to new clubs of men and women. We of the Speakers' Clubs, International, welcome you and wish you well. I will now call upon the District Service Manager of the International body to present to you the charter which will empower you to function as an affiliate.

PRESENTING CHARTER

After careful investigation of your petition for a charter to the Speakers' Clubs, International, your application has been approved. The Grand President has instructed me to form you into a chapter. It therefore gives me great pleasure to turn over to you the charter permitting you to func-

11

tion as a chapter of the Speakers' Clubs, International. The charter has been duly signed by the proper International officers. In turning over the charter to you permit me to say that you, who have been instrumental in the formation of this chapter, have undertaken an important task. Membership in this great organization of ambitious men and women is a privilege combined with responsibility. In every community there are men and women who would welcome the chance to secure such training if it were made available. Members of our Clubs will be found in public office, in the ranks of industry, in labor, in organizations of all kinds and among the leading businessmen and professionals.

You are now a regular chapter of the Speakers' Clubs, International. Therefore, the future of this chapter is the responsibility of its members. Be watchful of the character of those who seek admission, and if admitted, give them proper instruction and conduct the business of your chapter in accordance with the constitution and by-laws of the International.

By virtue of the dispensation granted by the Speakers' Clubs, International, I will proceed to install the officers to the end that they may function as the administrators of a duly instituted chapter of Speakers' Clubs, International. At the conclusion of the installation ceremonies, I will surrender this gavel to your president who will open the meeting and proceed to business. I wish to congratulate you on your enterprise in forming this chapter. We welcome you and hope you will thrive and prosper.

Closing

I express the hope that this newly formed Speakers' Club will endure for it has a useful purpose. It can be a great enterprise for good. It can serve you and will serve those yet to come. The opportunities afforded here will reinforce your capacity for leadership in the community, in your professions, in your lodges and clubs. It will provide opportunties for lasting friendships.

Affiliating with this Club means accepting an obligation to attend meetings and to accept and perform all assignments with diligence and sincerity. It involves research in the preparation for these assignments. It requires being well versed in community problems and national affairs. It means the development of hobbies and cultural interests.

I bid you farewell and the best of luck in your new enterprise.

B. ORGANIZING A CIVIC ASSOCIATION

OPENING BY TEMPORARY CHAIRMAN

We are embarking upon an important undertaking—the formation of an association of residents to protect and advance our interests and to stimulate a healthy participation in the civic affairs of our community. We cannot hope to be successful while working individually, but by combining our efforts the most beneficial results can be obtained. We are all bound together by a desire to achieve a better life and a better community for all. We have every hope that our common goal will be attained. This association of neighbors, now in the process of formation, needs your support, particularly at this stage of its development.

NOMINATION AND ELECTION OF OFFICERS

The first step in forming a group is to elect a president. Nominations are now in order. (*A motion is made to nominate John Jones for president. The nomination is seconded. Thereupon, it is regularly moved and seconded that nominations be closed.*)

There being no objection, nominations are closed and we shall proceed to vote. Please indicate your choice on the blank slips which are being handed out. (*Balloting proceeds and votes are counted.*)

I announce the result of the balloting is the unanimous election of John Jones. I therefore declare John Jones our first president. Mr. John Jones will now assume the chair (*temporary chairman retires*).

PRESIDENT'S ACCEPTANCE

Thank you for conferring upon me the honor of the presidency. I assure you that it is an honor which I appreciate deeply. Nothing could give me greater satisfaction than to be chosen the head of an organization of my neighbors. There are many matters of great concern to our community and it is reassuring to know that there is a group such as this to represent and speak for it.

NOMINATION AND ELECTION OF SECONDARY OFFICERS

We will now proceed to the nomination and election of the offices of vice-president, secretary, treasurer and an Executive Board, five members to serve for two years and five to serve for one year. (*A motion is made to cast a single ballot for the unanimous election of the entire slate. The motion is then seconded.*)

A motion having been made and seconded to cast a single ballot for the unanimous election of the slate which has been submitted by the Nominating Committee, I hereby instruct the secretary to cast a single ballot for the unanimous election of the persons nominated. (*Ballot is cast.*)

The Secretary having cast a ballot for the unanimous election of the slate, I hereby declare the persons nominated to be elected to their respective offices.

APPOINTING COMMITTEE TO DRAFT CONSTITUTION

I will appoint three members to draft a constitution and I instruct them to report at the next morning. (*Three members are designated.*)

ADJOURNING MEETING

If there is no objection the meeting will be adjourned. Hearing none, the meeting stands adjourned.

15

C. INSTALLING OFFICERS

OPENING

We are about to perform one of the most important rites incidental to our membership in the Speakers' Club—the installation of our newly elected officers.

The Speakers' Club is a non-profit organization which is designed to stimulate interest in and promote the art of cultural expression; it trains men and women in leadership; it stimulates and develops a greater interest in the art of public speaking and awakens a spirit of cooperation and friendship; it helps overcome intolerance and discrimination; it maintains an attitude strictly non-sectarian, non-partisan and non-sectional.

The Speakers' Club is more than an organization. It is a faith—a belief in democracy, a belief that men and women can assemble from different interests and occupations, from different social and economic conditions, and unite them for educational purposes and self-improvement.

INTRODUCING INSTALLING OFFICER

The installing officer, fittingly-enough, is a Past President of the Speakers' Club. He is the genial and able Charles Carter.

INSTALLING PRESIDENT

You have been chosen to preside over the destinies of the Speakers' Club for the ensuing year. The president is the most important person in the organization for upon him rests the responsibility of seeing that the club moves

16

forward and prospers. The honor of leadership carries with it responsibilities. The office is looked upon in most instances rightfully as a distinction and an honor, but it is primarily a post of service. You have won the confidence of the members and have been entrusted with this responsibility. You have been chosen as the person able to give most effective leadership. The president's obligation is to inspire our members, preserve peace and harmony and lead the club to success and accomplishment. A successful president is firm, competent, tactful and just. As I pass to you the gavel of your office, may I say that you possess all these qualifications and that you richly deserve the honor. I have every confidence in your ability to have a successful administration. The gavel is now yours. With it goes a warm welcome to our new leader and a pledge from every member to work with you toward even higher achievements.

INSTALLING VICE-PRESIDENT

Mr. Vincent Vale, our new Vice-President: The by-laws of the Speakers' Club require the Vice-President to perform all the duties of the president in his absence and to take the chair whenever he so requests. You are familiar with the powers and responsibilities of the president. Those powers and responsibilities are also yours. Your fellow members have found in you capabilities which will help our new president with the difficult and time-consuming tasks before him. We know you will be ever ready to assist him in the performance of his obligations.

INSTALLING TREASURER

Mr. Fred Fund, our new President: You are the guardian, the watchdog, of our funds. It is your duty prudently to manage the funds of the Club. The skillful performance of your duties is of the highest importance to the welfare and the prosperity of the organization.

INSTALLING SECRETARY

The secretary's duties are substantially of a business character and are of the highest importance to the welfare of the Club. Without a competent secretary the wheels of the Club would grind to a sudden stop. Punctuality in attendance at the meeting of the Club is an indispensable requisite of the secretary. He should be first in his place at its meetings, and the nature of his duties is such that he can scarcely avoid being the last to leave the meeting room. He is particularly charged with the duty of watching the proceedings of the Club and making a complete record of all things proper to be recorded; to keep the financial accounts between the Club and its members; to receive all moneys due to the Club and pay them into the hands of the treasurer; to prepare the annual reports and to perform all other duties pertaining to the office as may be ordered by the president.

INSTALLING EXECUTIVE BOARD

Board members are chosen for their qualifications of leadership for upon them depend the future strength and success of the organization. Board membership is an honor and a privilege and with it come responsibilities. The function of the Board is to look after the affairs of the organization between meetings. The Board is the team—the president, its captain. Good team-mates reap the reward of a smooth, soundly functioning organization.

INSTALLING RECORDING SECRETARY

Mr. Roy Wright, our new Recording Secretary: to you has been entrusted the keeping of the records of the Club.

Your reports and minutes constitute its current history. The recording secretary records the business transacted at all meetings and is the custodian of all documents and records. Your skill, understanding and judgment are well known to the members and we know the performance of the duties of your new office will make us even prouder of you.

ACCEPTANCE BY PRESIDENT

Thank you very much for the high honor you have conferred upon me. It is an honor of which any man may be proud. The roll of the ex-presidents of the Speakers' Club is an illustrious one. I have but two ambitions during my term of office: One is that I may be able to do as everyone of my predecessors has done, that is, leave the Club at the close of the term stronger and better than it was at the beginning; and my second ambition, that I may be able to call you all one year from tonight as I do not hesitate to call you all now—my personal friends.

CLOSING

In accepting leadership of the Speakers' Club, you, the new officers and board members have dedicated yourselves to the service of the members. Your choice as officers is a manifestation of the esteem in which you are held. We rejoice with you today. The members pledge to work untiringly at your side. I am confident that officers and members, hand in hand, will continue to meet their responsibilities with courage, with faith and with vision.

D. TESTIMONIAL TO JOURNALIST

OPENING

Freedom of the press, one of the most cherished cornerstones of our American heritage, was won before the Declaration of Independence. In 1773 John Peter Zenger, a New York printer, was imprisoned for taking issue with the British governor. Zenger's acquittal in a celebrated trial firmly established the precedent for a free and independent press in this land.

Today, we honor Roy Ralson for his efforts in preserving this heritage, for defending our liberty, for upholding our democratic principles, for keeping our press free, for his skillful and precisely accurate reporting of news. For all of these qualities he has been rightfully called the dean of reporters.

It is a great satisfaction to see that his wide knowledge, ability and devotion to public service are recognized by the tendering of this testimonial.

INTRODUCING JOURNALIST

We have with us to present an award to our guest-of-honor, a newspaper man whose honest interpretation of the news is known and respected by thousands. Many of us have benefitted from his clear and interesting accounts of important happenings of our times. He is a fearless champion of all that is good and right. Mr. Howard Hester.

PRESENTING AWARD

Every citizen of this community owes you a debt for the high civic service you have rendered to it. You have found time, despite exacting newspaper duties, to give your talents to welfare agencies. You are endowed with a fine mind, cultivated by unusual opportunities for mingling with people of distinction. Your untiring industry, your sound sense and unswerving fidelity have attracted attention. Your achievements are the result of inherent strength of character and intelligent application.

The Sun-Journal is establishing a Roy Ralson Award for distinguished service to journalism to be given to members of the organization who show unusual enterprise and initiative. You are the first to receive such an award. We recognize fully the service you have rendered to our organization. No one deserves the plaque more than you do. Therefore, on behalf of the Sun-Journal organization it is my privilege to present to you the Roy Ralson Award for truly outstanding work and distinguished service; for your contribution to humanity through journalism; for your fight for the elimination of discrimination by reason of race or creed; for your reputation as a fearless fighter for the good of the people. There are few who would state the truth more bluntly or with less fear of consequences—or shout it louder than you.

This dinner also gives the public an opportunity to recognize the efforts of their local newspapermen—those hardworking craftsmen who regularly channel into the lives about them the most important and humanly interesting happenings of the times. The role of the press as an agency of public education is an important one. Newspaper week deserves to be universally observed.

I am happy to pay this tribute to you. It is a great privilege for me to salute so distinguished a journalist, the dean of newspapermen.

INTRODUCING GUEST-OF-HONOR

I now give you the man you have been waiting to hear. Roy is favorably known to public officials, diplomats and correspondents abroad and at home. His warm personality and capacity for friendship serves him well in the gathering of news and the development of news sources. He is a man of great qualities—integrity, balance, common sense, courage, simplicity, a high sense of civic duty. He has had long experience in public life and many contacts with world statesmen. World figures admired him and put their confidence in him, as did his newspaper colleagues. He has political know-how and considerable popular appeal. He is one of the most talented in the field of journalism. His many years with the Sun-Journal have brought that newspaper to a position of great prestige and influence. And now our guest-of-honor, Roy Ralson.

THANKS AND APPRECIATION

I am deeply touched by the fact that so many have done me the honor to come out tonight. I want to thank you at the outset, Mr. Jameson, for the wonderful manner in which you have presided at this testimonial dinner. I deem it a very great honor for me to be the first recipient of the Roy Ralson award. Please don't get the idea that you owe me a debt. I enjoyed the various positions I have held with the paper for so many years. I have been happy in the practice of my profession. No one can hold those positions I have held without becoming deeply interested in the work of the newspaper.

I have written a few remarks for this occasion but no script can prepare one for the emotions I feel at this moment. It is difficult to find words to express my thanks for the kind thoughts—the confidence in me that was expressed tonight. The words of praise and tribute are pleas-

22

ing but at the same time they serve to emphasize the great responsibility that will be mine to live up to.

William Shakespeare, who obviously found himself as hard-put as I am now for words to match your kind sentiments, said:

"I can no other answer make but thanks
And thanks, and ever thanks"

And thus "thanks and thanks and ever thanks" for the kindness you have shown me—for the confidence you have placed in me.

CLOSING

Everything that has been said about Roy Ralson has been well said. We all wish him happiness, and it is our fervent hope that the honor and happiness which he and his family are now enjoying may continue and increase for the rest of his days.

E. TESTIMONIAL TO PHILANTHROPIST

Opening

It is a matter of pride and pleasure to pay tribute to a man whose activities have found him in the forefront of all communal endeavors. He has dedicated his superb talents to the furtherance of human welfare. He is a founder, director and general benefactor of the Mercy Hospital and one of the mainstays of the institution. His great interest and steady counsel have been a constant source of strength. He is a leader in many other charitable endeavors and has a long and brilliant record of support and active participation on behalf of the sick, aged and troubled.

We are proud to have such a man among us—proud to do him the honor he so richly deserves. His sympathetic understanding of civic needs, his vision and attainments have enriched our community. This dinner is for the purpose of expressing our heartfelt thanks to Richard Stone for the inspiration of his example.

Introducing Donor of Citation

I present to you one who is indefatigable in his devotion to problems of public welfare, a leader for many years in virtually every aspect of the public good, who is constantly expanding his horizons and is devoted to the interests of Mercy Hospital. Mr. John Smith.

Presenting the Citation

Mr. Richard Stone, the evidences of your philanthropies appear throughout this community. You helped build the

Mercy Hospital, the Youth Center and many other monuments of your self-sacrificing devotion to the community. You have helped the present campaign with your usual zeal. It is my privilege on behalf of the Committee to present to you this illuminated and engraved citation which tells of your generosity to the community. I will read the citation:

> "The contribution he has made to the health, welfare and well-being of his fellow citizens and his contribution to the great humanitarian enterprises of our generation have been in keeping with the dictates of a warm and understanding generosity; he has given years of devoted service to civic and philanthropic causes."

It is with deep pride that we pay this tribute to an outstanding leader and friend. Your interest and devotion to the welfare of your fellow-man has set a precedent of community responsibility, philanthropy and brotherhood which serves as an inspiration for all of us. We, the members of the committee, are happy to have this opportunity to express publicly our high regard to a friend and colleague, and show our admiration for your life and work.

I join in congratulations on your splendid record of achievements made possible by hard and steady adherence to high ideals and American traditions.

GUEST-OF-HONOR ACKNOWLEDGES PRAISE AND CITATION

I am deeply grateful for the honor you have done me in presenting to me this beautiful citation. Life affords a man few joys more sweet than appreciation by his neighbors and colleagues. Your tributes and the award of this citation have moved me more than I can tell you. Let me add that I have done nothing more than to serve the community in my own humble way as best I could. I shall continue to serve as long as I am able. Thank you very much for everything.

CLOSING

I think it is altogether fitting that on an occasion like this we reflect on the achievements of Richard Stone. By dint of hard work and the possession of a congenial personality he won success in business, friends and recognition. He had little to start with except a large amount of courage and a great deal of faith in an ideal.

F. TESTIMONIAL ON RETIREMENT OF PUBLIC OFFICIAL

OPENING

There are few men in public life of whom it could be said with more feeling on the eve of their retirement: "Well done, thou good and faithful servant," than of Senator Charles Jones. It is inspiring to know that politics can produce public servants such as he has proved himself to be. His long and distinguished career has added lustre and distinction to the Senate. He has served his community beyond appraisal. Senator Jones is one of the voices in the Senate that could always be counted upon to speak up for justice, for decency and for dignity. He has done much to humanize our laws and bring its rules into harmony with the economic conditions of this age. The Senate will sorely miss him.

We hope he will have many more years. His unselfish devotion to public causes merits the tributes he will receive tonight.

INTRODUCING DONOR OF GIFT

I present to you a distinguished member of the community who occupies a position of respect and influence as our village mayor. He has been asked by the committee in charge to make a presentation to our guest-of-honor. It is my pleasure to introduce Mayor Samuel Smith.

PRESENTING GOLD CUP

Senator Jones' retirement provides a welcome opportunity to pay tribute to his accomplishments and to his many services to our community. Rare indeed is the man who can point to a quarter century of selfless devotion to his fellow-man. His 25 years of service gives us all a chance to celebrate his deeds, reflect on his wise guidance and to toast his outspoken courage, steadfastness and devotion.

His wealth of experience and knowledge, his large acquaintance and great popularity have made him an outstanding personality. His efforts on behalf of our community have contributed more than any other thing to its progress and welfare. As a token of our affection, the committee has recommended that we take some definite action in reference to his retirement beyond the simple statement of appreciation. We thought we would give him something to place in his home or office to remember the good-will of this organization. We are, therefore, presenting to him a gold cup as a measure of the esteem in which he is held. And I may add that if this cup were as big as this room, all of the good wishes of our membership would fill it to overflowing. And so, on behalf of the Executive Board, I present to you, Senator Jones, this gold cup with engraved inscription on it:

> "Awarded to Senator Charles Jones for his distinguished service in advancing the health, education and welfare of the people of the community."

THANKING SPEAKER

I am sure that our guest-of-honor will always recall with a glow of pride and satisfaction the tribute paid to him by Mayor Smith and the presentation of the gold cup.

Introducing Public Official

It is with unalloyed pleasure that I present to you the great Governor of our great State. He needs no words of introduction or praise from me. The effectiveness of his administration is the highest commendation that he can receive. I present Governor Steven Stone.

Address of Tribute

I am pleased indeed to join in the tributes to Senator Charles Jones and to extend to him my heartiest best wishes on the occasion of his retirement from official life. Although I have known for some time that for personal reasons he would not continue his services to the Senate, I am indeed sorry that he finds it necessary at this time to return to private life. However, now that he has made his decision I am glad to salute his contributions and wish him well.

Senator Jones, you retire to private life with the satisfaction of knowing that you have made a substantial contribution to the welfare of your community and state.

Public service not infrequently demands of those who seek its rewards the possession of many good qualities and virtues. None of your colleagues will forget your wise counsel and calm confidence in the face of every kind of difficulty —your concern for the welfare of the people—the warm heart as well as the skill you brought to every job. You have carried a heavy burden of responsibilities in a job where brickbats usually outnumber thanks. But it is only necessary to remember the number of good laws on the statute books which you authored to know that you deserve a big hand for work well done. You have never considered your personal comfort or interests when it was necessary to correct an evil condition. No man could more readily than you understand the range of a problem and go right to the core.

It is my distinct pleasure to salute you, Senator, and wish you good health, good luck and the best of everything.

THANKING SPEAKER

Thank you, Governor Stone, for taking time out of a very busy schedule to come here to pay tribute to our guest-of-honor. We, in the community, can rejoice that Senator Jones' wise counsel, experience and courage still will be available to us. When we appeal to him for assistance, as we are bound to do, it will be a comfort to know that his talents will be at our disposal.

INTRODUCING GUEST-OF-HONOR

Without further ado, I present our guest-of-honor who I know will want to respond to the things that have been said about him. Senator Charles Jones.

RESPONSE BY GUEST-OF-HONOR

I am quite overwhelmed. I find it hard to express my gratitude. First, I must acknowledge the very generous and lavish praise and thank you for your display of affection and friendship. I am particularly happy so many of you could come. I am deeply moved and complimented by your gift of a gold cup commemorating my retirement from public life. Truly, my cup of happiness runneth over. No gift could be more appreciated or give me greater joy. I thank the Governor for his presence here and for his fine tribute and I would like him to know that it was an honor to have served with a man whose life has been devoted to the people of the state. To Mayor Smith, my sincerest thanks for all that he has so extravagantly said about my accomplishments and to Fred Fund for the excellent manner in which he presided at this wonderful dinner and to each of you for the courtesy you have shown me by coming here tonight that I might greet you. Above all, I should pay a salute to my wife, Jane, for all she did to make my political career possible—for her fortitude, her faith, her magnificent courage, her insistence on simplicity in all things—my debt to her is very great. It only remains that I should say, not goodbye—I do not want to say that—but goodnight, and God bless you.

CLOSING

Senator, you well deserve the words of praise and appreciation voiced here tonight. I predict for you the same success in private life that you have enjoyed in your many years of distinguished public service. We are happy that you will continue your activities in the community and that we will frequently see you here. God bless you and aid all of your endeavors.

G.   DEDICATING HOME FOR AGED

OPENING

The Reverend Paul Paulson will invoke the Divine Blessing.

DIVINE BLESSING

Almighty God, we beseech Thee, for all who are devoted to the betterment of humanity, broaden our horizons so that we may see that the goal of life is greater than bread and meat, and help us realize that all men are our brothers. Hasten the day of peace and concord in world affairs, we pray Thee, and grant us peace and happiness for all generations.

GREETING AND WELCOME

I deeply appreciate the privilege of presiding at these ceremonies. The opening of the Home for the Aged has been a goal for which we have worked, planned and sacrificed. All of us should applaud the committee, the many workers and contributors, for this dream-come-true. The community has made a good beginning toward recognizing their responsibility to the elderly citizens. It is a monument to those who have envisioned it and then made the vision come true. Our institutions which are designed for a shorter life span are inadequate, outworn and outmoded. The Home will be staffed by personnel trained in geriatric problems. The Home for the Aged will render service on the basis of human dignity and individual worth. No guest will ever pay a cent to the Home.

32

INTRODUCING COMMITTEE CHAIRMAN

The Chairman of the Building Committee has served with energy and effectiveness and with the same zeal that he has displayed in all other positions undertaken during his distinguished career. His love for this edifice is so strong that all his waking moments have been spent hastening the day when its facilities would be made available to those who need them. I present Brother Fulton Fund.

DEDICATORY ADDRESS

I appreciate the honor of being permitted to take part in the dedication of this fine Home. I am sure that everyone here is impressed by its beautiful setting and sturdy construction.

The test of the conscience of a community is in its attitude toward its aged, its distressed and its sick. Today that test is being met intelligently.

We are here to dedicate this new Home. In one sense we cannot dedicate a building to anything. It remains stone. In reality we are here to re-dedicate ourselves as members of the community. This building is but a symbol—the outward manifestation of an idea and an ideal. The Home we are dedicating memorializes our responsibility to the community.

The care of our aging is one of our obligations. The obligation applies to us individually and collectively. Our elders must be kept healthy and happy. It is not only a real joy to be able to take care of those who cared for us and brought us to this time of our lives, but it is our responsibility.

We publicly express sincere thanks to the great many people who aided in bringing about the completion of this great work. We are grateful to the civic, religious and social groups which helped in this project—to the many men and women of the community who by their contributions made possible this magnificent event. The community owes a special debt of gratitude to the men and women who envisioned this Home for the Aged. It is fitting to dedicate this structure to them in grateful acknowledgment of a debt for which there can be no repayment.

I felt signally honored when the presiding officer invited me to help dedicate the edifice. But my pleasure was immeasurably increased when I was asked to make a presentation of the building key to Mr. Roy Rankin, the President of the Board of Directors of the Home for the Aged.

PRESENTING BUILDING KEY

This key which opens the door to a much needed refuge for our senior citizens has little intrinsic value. It is merely a symbol. After you have received it, Mr. Rankin, you will, no doubt, put it away never to use again. The doors of this beautiful structure will always be open to all aged and needy applicants of the community regardless of race or creed. The door will not be closed to any of them. I now present this key to you with the knowledge that it opens the door to the best care modern medical knowledge can devise and the generosity of the members of the community can afford.

ACCEPTING BUILDING KEY

On behalf of the Home for the Aged and its Board of Directors, I acknowledge and accept this building key to the Home. I accept it with a deep sense of responsibility. This new building can be no more than a prologue. We have built only a doorway and our obligation today is to look forward through it. This Home is an expression of faith in private initiative in the field of human welfare.

I am confident that a grateful community will find means to maintain this splendid institution. Whether we can open the doors even wider will depend upon their generosity. Certainly, we take pride in the fulfillment of our determination to have so fine a Home for the Aged as this we are dedicating. The Home we are dedicating provides the elderly with recreation and activity facilities which will give them a feeling of usefulness and belonging, of adequacy and accomplishment. It is worthy of the support of the community. We are fully cognizant of the unselfishness of the civic, religious and labor organizations in meeting the physical, emotional and spiritual needs of the aging who will spend their sunset years in the Home. This is indeed a public service and a humanitarian contribution to our society. The Home memorializes the community's responsibility to the aging.

It is fitting to dedicate this structure to our civic, religious and labor organizations in grateful acknowledgment for its work.

CONSECRATION PRAYER

Almighty and everlasting God, who governs all things in heaven and earth, mercifully hear the supplications of Thy people, and grant us peace all the days of our life. Most heartily we beseech Thee, to behold and bless our aged and ailing and so replenish them with the grace of Thy Holy Spirit that they may always incline to Thy will and walk in Thy Way. Endow them plenteously with heavenly gifts; grant them in health and happiness long to live. Almighty God, graciously enable us now to dedicate this house which we have erected to the honor and glory of

Thy name, and be mercifully pleased to accept this service at our hands. Amen!

In the name of the community which envisioned this project, we do solemnly dedicate this Home.

CLOSING

What at its inception was considered by many as somewhat of a dream has now become a reality. This fine building is a tribute to the foresight, planning and cooperation of the members of the community. Today, we make good a promise to the community and to ourselves. This Home fills a real community need.

The problem of our aging keeps mounting as the life span increases. We are determined to give our aging a Home and the best care that modern medical knowledge can devise. We assumed that obligation as members of the community.

However, this is just the beginning. Our obligation is a continuing one. The Home must be properly maintained. Older persons are more apt to be disabled and succumb to illnesses. When sick or disabled, older persons remain sick or disabled for longer periods. The need for hospitalization is greater among older persons.

The great debt which society owes to our older citizens for all their years of service we are helping to repay in this very fine way.

H. DEDICATING RECREATION CENTER

GREETING AND WELCOME

We have gathered today for a momentous occasion. The dedication of the Recreation Center has great significance for the welfare and progress of our community. It is a great pleasure to welcome you to these dedication ceremonies. I present Bishop Ernest Land who has graciously consented to deliver the opening prayer.

INVOCATION

Almighty and Everlasting God, vouchsafe we beseech Thee to direct, sanctify and govern both our hearts and bodies in the ways of Thy laws and in the works of Thy commandments that through Thy most merciful being we may be preserved in body and soul. Direct us, O Lord, in all our doings with Thy most gracious favor that in all our works begun, continued and ended in Thee, we may glorify Thy holy name, and finally, by Thy mercy obtain everlasting life. Amen!

INTRODUCING SPEAKER

I present to you a man who has at all times been interested in problems of our youth. His philosophy of government and approach to civic problems are notable for their clarity and humanitarianism. He has led the fight for such objectives as more parks, better schools, improved child-care programs, good housing and racial cooperation. He is a symbol of the intelligent, informed and independent legislator. With profound satisfaction, I present Congressman Frank Smith.

DEDICATORY ADDRESS

This marks a significant step in the fulfillment of a dream. This organization may indeed be proud of the role it has taken for the betterment of the community. It has made a real contribution to the solution of a current problem. It should be stressed from the beginning that the work being done is preventive not corrective. The youngsters to be served are good boys from good families. They deserve every opportunity to remain so. Recreation centers and their personnel give boys that chance. They provide whole-sale fun for their leisure time, healthful outlets for their excess energy, proper instruction and the opportunity to play at competitive sports, to acquire useful hobbies and to learn skills and handicrafts. They provide playgrounds, ballfields and club houses.

Great effort and thought, as well as much money, have gone into the erection of this Recreation Center. Your contributions will add immeasurably to the happiness of neighborhood youngsters and the well-being of our entire community. The success of the enterprise is dependent upon continuous, dedicated and highly skilled effort.

It is my solemn privilege to dedicate this edifice which is a silent memorial of our responsibility to the community. What the destiny of this structure shall be is in our hands. May the Supreme Architect of the Universe guide us and give us divine assistance in lifting our hearts, our souls, to greater heights for the welfare of all His children!

THANKING SPEAKER

We owe much to the unflagging interest and support by Congressman Smith in community affairs. This Recreation Center, which he has so impressively dedicated, is only one of the many causes he sponsors. The community is proud of you, Congressman.

CLOSING

This is a big day for the entire community especially for the workers who toiled to bring this dream to realization. This is only a beginning but a proud one. This community has a challenging opportunity for service in the years ahead. You have shown that you are ready to meet the challenge. This Center should repay its costs many times over in building good citizens. It is a doorway through which a growing child can be made aware that here is understanding, sympathy and a friendly interest.

The dedication of our Recreation Center represents a great opportunity for members of our community to render service. It has taken bold and courageous planning to bring to its fruition this magnificent Recreation Center. It has been worth it. To say that we have reached our goal would be misleading, but the summit is in sight. It is hoped that the community will continue their efforts on behalf of this great humanitarian project. What remains to be done is to make funds available for several years of unbroken maintenance of our Recreation Center. The campaign is continuing and the work to be done is just as important and necessary as that just completed.

The work of the members of the Building Committee cannot be compensated fully by words of praise. I, as chairman, can only say that without them the task would have been impossible.

I. CORNERSTONE DEDICATION

OPENING

We have convened to lay the foundation stones of the Youth Center. The edifice to be built on this site will be devoted to the promotion of character development, citizenship training and physical and spiritual fitness of the youth of the area. The Center when completed will provide wholesome recreation and social opportunities for boys and girls.

It is the custom upon occasions like the present to deposit beneath the cornerstone certain items of significance of the period in which it was laid. The various articles composing the deposit are here safely enclosed and comprise copies of all local newspapers, several current magazines and a brochure describing the edifice which is to be erected here. I now deposit these articles beneath the cornerstone.

DEDICATION PRAYER

Almighty God, by whom all things are made, grant that whatever shall be builded on this stone may be to Thy glory and the honor of Thy great name.

PROCLAMATION

I now proclaim that this cornerstone has been laid.

INTRODUCING SPEAKER

The dedicatory address will be made by one who has worked hard and diligently in initiating this project and can be counted on to see it through to completion—Mr. Frank Ball.

CORNERSTONE LAYING ADDRESS

The building of this Youth Center and its maintenance is an undertaking worth supporting. It is a useful and fruitful work. It would be more humane and ultimately more economical to try to understand the causes of youth's defiance and eradicate them. It is impossible to point to any quick cure. There are, however, at least several areas upon which thought and attention should be focused. Everything which restores to the young person the sense of belonging, of having responsibilities and being wanted are steps in the right direction. Churches, social agencies, block-by-block groups—in short, the whole complex of community life, must pull together to restore to youth the awareness of a deep interest in him. The problem is great and touches our society at the heart. The work we are doing here goes to the "hard core" of the problem.

This building, when completed, will be a monument to the sense of responsibility of the community. Here it will stand, we hope, a long, long time, saying to all citizens that we mean to work long and patiently for the benefit of our young people.

The facilities of this Youth Center will be used by the children of the neighborhood without charge and without distinction of color or creed. Because of the generosity of the people of this community, it is possible to offer these facilities. We are truly proud of the community spirit which has initiated a project so much needed.

The speed with which this Center is completed will depend largely on the flow of contributions from donors to provide $200,000 to make the new institution a reality.

I know that the citizens of this community who initiated this splendid project will see it through to a speedy and successful completion. These ceremonies are promises that no youth shall be denied his birthright of a good childhood.

PRESENTING TROWEL

I have been asked to perform a very pleasant duty before closing, and that is to present to Mayor Samuel Smith this silver trowel as a memento of this occasion. The inscription on the trowel commemorates this event and bears the names of all the civic, social, school, and religious organizations of the community sponsoring the Youth Center. The honor is rightfully his for all he has done for the community and for this project. I am proud to have been designated as the one to present this to you, Mayor Smith.

CLOSING

We will conclude the ceremonies with an appropriate prayer by Reverend George Green.

PRAYER

May the Supreme Architect of the Universe guard and bless this place and prosper all the laudable works of those connected with it! May He protect the craftsmen employed in this work from every harm. May our country continue in peace and prosperity throughout all generations. Amen!

J. MEMORIAL SERVICES

OPENING

We have gathered here to pay our tribute of farewell to the distinguished and revered Henry Hart, our beloved and esteemed colleague. He was a courageous champion of justice and freedom. His faith in God was unswerving. His devotion to America was strong and impassioned. He was a many-sided citizen. This community particularly owes much to Harry Hart for his aggressive and devoted toil in behalf of cultural and civic welfare and for his interfaith philanthropies. He held many positions of trust, confidence and honor. He was a man of rare personal attraction, of a genial, generous nature, full of kindness. He went out of his way to help friends. He asked no favors for himself.

I am sure that many of you who are present would like, after the prayer, to make appropriate expression of your feelings.

PRAYER

Almighty Father, in sorrow and gratitude we would give Thee thanks for all the contributions and achievements of this Thy servant, Henry Hart, to the life of our community. He was of noble spirit, possessed of humanitarian principles and with a compassionate understanding of the suffering. His high moral integrity, lofty ideals, broad sympathies and unselfish devotion to democratic principles won for him the love and affection of the community. He was saintly in character, liberal in spirit and vigorous in mind. He had a love of people and an immense respect for the worth and dignity of the individual. He was endowed with a fine

43

mind. He was kind and generous, and his manners were stamped with the gentleness and honesty of his nature. His fidelity and loyalty to his friends was one of his greatest traits. In his death the community has lost one of its principal leaders.

INTRODUCING PUBLIC OFFICIAL

I present one of the honored gentlemen of this community. He has reached a position of prestige, respect and influence in public life. His position was attained by a solid faith in three great bulwarks of our way of life— faith in God, faith in America and faith in his fellow-man. Wherever the cause of freedom is treasured his name is held in admiration and respect. Senator Samuel Shield.

EULOGY

We have sustained a grievous loss with the passing of our beloved friend Henry Hart. It is difficult to estimate our loss. The world we live in seems poorer and less hopeful without him. There is no disguising the fact that the death of Henry Hart is a heavy misfortune for us and our community.

It was my good fortune to know Henry Hart intimately. He radiated from his personality a charm and sweetness. As we go through this busy life each striving selfishly to survive, becoming callous to the feelings of our fellows—it is remarkable to meet a personality like that of Henry Hart. I know that the impress he left upon me is a durable one. I found him to be one of nature's noblemen. He touched nothing that he didn't brighten and better. I don't think there is any man who came in contact with him who didn't add to his own determination to be better and more sympathetic and generous to his fellowman.

He distinguished himself by his sincere dedication and substantial contribution to the welfare of his community. His spirit of humanity, of devotion to the good of all, carried over into all fields of endeavor, including charitable and philanthropic activities. His passing leaves a void in our hearts and in the community that will be difficult to fill. I extend my personal sympathies to his bereaved wife and family.

ANNOUNCEMENT

The Secretary of the Association of which Henry Hart was a former president will read a resolution of sympathy.

RESOLUTION OF SYMPATHY

WHEREAS the passing of our former president HENRY HART instills in our hearts a feeling of deep sorrow, and

WHEREAS the late HENRY HART distinguished himself by his sincere dedication and substantial contribution to the welfare of the community, be it

RESOLVED that we, the officers and members of the Association, deeply regret the passing of our former president HENRY HART and do hereby offer our sincere and heartfelt sympathy and condolence to his beloved wife and family.

FURTHER RESOLVED that a copy of this resolution be sent to the family of the late HENRY HART.

CLOSING

The only thing I can say in concluding is that we are consoled by the thought of a memory so beautiful and so wonderful, of a life so clean and so decent, of a character so elevated, that I am sure his family and friends will remember him long after this sorrowful and sad occasion. And in this sad moment, perhaps we may repeat these words of Philip James Bailey:

"We live in deeds, not years; in thoughts,
    not breath;
In feelings, not in figures on a dial,
We should count time by heart-throbs.
He most lives who thinks most, feels the
    noblest, acts the best."

By those standards, no life was fuller than Henry Hart's.
The Lord in his love hath given, the Lord in His own
judgment hath taken away. Blessed be the name of God!

K. VETERANS DAY OBSERVANCE

OPENING OF COMMEMORATIVE SERVICES

The hour of eleven having arrived, it is appropriate that we pause in meditation and silent prayer for our noble men who sacrificed their lives to maintain our highest traditions. This is a solemn day when every American should give thanks to those who have done so much to make possible the way of life we cherish.

Let us bow our heads in silent prayer for everlasting peace. Let us pray that in our troubled world a road will be found to lasting peace—a kind that will go on and on. The battle will not be won until the whole wide world lives beneath a brilliant peaceful sun.

PRAYER

May the Lord permit His countenance to shine upon those who made the supreme sacrifice and upon this land and the ideals for which they gave their lives.

Let us give thanks for those who found this land, and shaped America, and made us what we are; for the men and women, living and dead, known and unknown, who have spoken the thoughts we shared, who have sung the songs we knew who have built the things we dreamed.

MEMORIAL ADDRESS

This occasion is one of great national symbolism. It is dedicated to those men, living and dead, who served in all our wars. This day was set aside to honor all the veterans

47

who have fought to keep the flag of freedom flying over this our cherished land.

On this day we renew our dedication to the eternal quest for the Holy Grail of lasting peace, not for ourselves alone, but for all mankind.

Let us pray for peace, but be prepared for war. We dedicate ourselves to be prepared to defend ourselves against aggression. We do not glorify war.

Veterans Day, with its memories of past wars, presents no more forceful lesson than that America must always face the future on guard, with the power to defend maintained at a realistic and effective level.

We meet here every year to express our debt to those who served; to express our pride in the valor of America's sons and daughters; to show our pride in the ideals for which they fought.

On this day we reaffirm the nation's obligation to all those who went into the Valley of the Shadow of Death. Our nation has never and must never neglect its obligation to honor those who died, to care for those who received lasting injury, are ill and destitute.

I now dedicate this monument to those who gave all they were and all they had to the cause of freedom. I will read the inscription etched on this monument:

"In reverend recognition of the Divine Guidance and to the eternal memory of those who gave the last full measure of devotion to their country, this monument is dedicated humbly to their sacrifices in defense of our freedoms."

This monument will serve to keep alive and fresh and vigorous our appreciation of their greatness. We observe Veterans Day as one of remembrance.

CLOSING

Today will recall to many an unhappy recollection—Pearl Harbor Day—a day that will stand forever as the symbol of lack of vigilance, a dark reminder that our dereliction cost many young men their lives. Firmly, we resolve that this must never happen again. Never again must the enemy be permitted to catch us unguarded. This is a day, however, when we recall our debt to the war disabled—when we can resolve they must never be permitted to believe their sacrifices were in vain, or forgotten.

L. PHYSICIAN-OF-THE-YEAR AWARD

OPENING

We have been brought together to honor and pay tribute to a benefactor of the community. Our guest-of-honor came to this community 30 years ago. His untiring industry, sound sense and unswerving fidelity soon attracted attention and he rapidly acquired a large practice. Whoever sought his services and followed his advice did not fail to profit by it. His success is the result of inherent strength of character and intelligent application. His zeal and devotion to his community have never failed or faltered. Whenever an individual or organization devoted to helping people needed help, our guest-of-honor could always be counted on.

It is a wonderful privilege for us to see Dr. Robert Bookman publicly rewarded—to see his merits openly appreciated.

INTRODUCING LAWYER

The legal counterpart of our guest-of-honor, who is his life-long friend, has come here to pay tribute to him. Like our guest-of-honor, his roots are deep in his community. He too serves on the school board, heads the charity drives and is a man of action whenever the community needs leadership. It is my honor to present Mr. Richard Blackstone.

TRIBUTES

Our friend and physician, Dr. Robert Bookman, is a man of science, learning and skill. His profound knowledge and experience have won for him widespread recognition in his profession. Like many men of accomplishment he is unaffected and unassuming. By his integrity and great learning he has earned for himself a place of great distinction in the community.

During his long and very active career, Dr. Bookman has been called upon by his fellow-citizens to take a prominent part in many civic crises and movements. He participated in nearly every campaign to raise funds. His position as a leader among physicians is recognized by the members of his profession in the area and, undoubtedly, the community regards him as a great doctor. His views on the community problems as they arose are the views of a patriotic and honorable citizen and a man of high character, bigness of heart and warmth of personality.

Dr. Bookman is known for his unfailing courtesy to everyone. Every patient who enters his office finds in him a friend and an inspiration. This sketch would not be complete without an illusion to his charitable disposition. He is connected with every community enterprise which has for its object the alleviation of suffering and the relief of the poor and the afflicted. Together with Mrs. Bookman he helped to establish and support the Home of the Aged. He is a subscriber to many other charitable organizations. To his task of repairing sick bodies he brings not only a sound medical background but an unquenchable enthusiasm and an affection for his patients which obviously help in their recovery. His sense of humor is also on tap for those who are tense and worried. It is very proper that such a man who does so much to maintain the honor and dignity of the medical profession should merit the public appreciation of the community and the designation "Physician-of-the-Year."

INTRODUCING SPEAKER FOR PRESENTATION

The person who has been chosen to make a presentation to our guest-of-honor is active in all things benefiting humanity. His theory of life is that he is going to pass this way but once and if, in passing, he can add any pleasure to the lives of those he met, he would do it, and he is doing it. He loves people and people love him. I present with pleasure, a friend of our guest-of-honor, Mr. William Church.

PRESENTING HONORARY MEMBERSHIP CARD

I have a very pleasant duty to perform and that is to present to Dr. Robert Bookman a tangible reminder of the affection we have for him. We would like Dr. Bookman to honor us as we would honor him. We would like him to become one of us in this organization.

What I say of Bob is not from hearsay but a close friendship with him for more than 20 years. He is a man who is devoted to his family, his profession, his community. He is an able, painstaking and conscientious doctor. Nothing can turn him aside from the path he has marked for himself. He has no desire for ease or the accumulation of great wealth. Bob has taken an active part in every welfare program of this community and has aided every fund-raising drive. He impresses everyone with his physical and mental vigor and energy. Dr. Bookman is a man of vitality and imagination who attained eminence in his profession and in the community. It is, therefore, my cherished privilege to present to him this gold honorary membership card which is inscribed:

"Presented to Dr. Robert Bookman, Physcian-of-the-Year, in grateful appreciation for all he has done for the needy and afflicted. The call of duty has never gone unanswered. To his patients he gives his best efforts, the benefit of his wide knowledge, large experience and untiring diligence."

This community owes Dr. Bookman a great debt. In a small way a doctor shares the lives of a great many people. He knows their troubles, worries with them, does his best to make them well and happy and is glad with them when he succeeds. A good doctor is, within the limits of his own field, the servant of the humblest individual who needs his services. Dr. Bookman has been many things to the members of our community and we are grateful.

I hope that the years to come will bring him the best of health and happiness.

ACCEPTING HONOR AND ACKNOWLEDGING TRIBUTES

It would be quite unnatural if I were not deeply touched by this evidence of your good-will. I am proud to be the recipient of this Gold Membership Card and I accept it with gratitude and a deep sense of humility. It is because this gift from you implies that I am considered worthy that I will treasure and hold it dearly.

I have really done nothing more than in my own humble way to serve this fine community as best I could. I shall continue to serve as long as I am able. Any doctor who is even moderately active sees in the course of a year several hundred patients. In my years of practice, I have had many people tell me of their sicknesses, anxieties and problems. From this store of experience I have learned that every man, woman and child, regardless of his station in life, regardless of racial origin, is worthy of and should be treated with respect, as befits the essential dignity of man.

I want to thank my friend Bill Church for his fine presentation and Dick Blackstone for his very generous tributes and our chairman for his excellent conduct of the meeting. I cannot tell you the pleasure I feel in being an honorary member of this great Association. The work of the Association is such as to deserve real commendation for its efforts in building better communities.

CLOSING

Doc Bookman is a most useful citizen and a great friend of the sick. We hope his works and his warmth will be with us for many years to come.

We will conclude with the delivery by Reverend Lake of the well known and inspiring prayer by Charles Lewis Slattery.

CLOSING PRAYER

"Almighty God, we thank Thee for the job of this day; may we find gladness in all its toil and difficulty, in its pleasure and success, and even in its failure and sorrow. We would look always away from ourselves, and behold the glory and the need of the world that we may have the will and the strength to bring the gift of gladness to others; that with them, we may stand to bear the burden and heat of the day and offer Thee the praise of work well done. Amen."

M. BROTHERHOOD AWARD

GREETING AND WELCOME

May I extend a sincere welcome to you on the occasion of
the presentation of the Brotherhood Award to Chester
Snow. Each year we award to a worthy individual a citation
for effective work in advancing understanding among
the groups that comprise America. We regard these annual
presentations as an occasion for planning for the future
rather than a reason for tabulating past successes and
accomplishments. Not that we intend to ignore them but
what lies ahead is challenging and provocative. I am confident that all of you will help to make the coming years an
era of solid progress.

Chester Snow, whom we honor today, has an unparalleled
love for human beings. He has been active in stimulating
educational programs for justice, amity, understanding and
co-operation among all peoples. He has done much to
alleviate, and where possible, eliminate the prejudices which
disfigure and distort business, social and political relation-
ships among our citizens. He is truly a good citizen. He has
our esteem, our respect and our affection.

INTRODUCING CIVIL LIBERTIES CHAMPION

Our speaker is endowed with courage, vision, ability,
and a profound faith in humanity. His compassion, his
understanding, his love, embraces all mankind, regardless
of sect, or creed, or race. We need men such as he and
Chester Snow, to build a better world, a world of peace and
human brotherhood and mutual understanding among peo-

ples. It is my privilege to introduce to you, Dr. Freeman
Frank.

PRESENTING SCROLL

I can only heavily underscore what the toastmaster has
said about Chester Snow. I speak as one member of the
community who is fortunate to enjoy his friendship and
companionship. He has made a tremendous contribution
to the welfare of this community. There are few who show
a more understanding love of their fellow-man. His interest
in public affairs is great. One of Mr. Snow's achievements—
in which he takes special pride—is the establishment in
the community of a Conference of the various religious
faiths designed to stimulate understanding. He has pro-
moted a strictly educational program for understanding and
co-operation among the religious groups that comprise the
community and has fortified efforts for a better world for all
men.

It is entirely fitting that this scroll be awarded to a man
whose distinguished career stands as a shining example for
all of us to try to follow. It is, therefore, my cherished
privilege to present to you, Chester Snow, this citation
which reads:

"For more than ten years, Chester Snow gave to
the movement to encourage good-will among
American racial and religious groups leadership,
encouragement and inspiration. The fight for civil
rights is a never ending one and has seldom de-
manded more courage and steadfastness than during the years when Mr. Snow headed the Committee for Promotion of Brotherhood. Those high
traits he possesses in full measure and has displayed them always as our devoted chairman.

"With insight into the needs and processes of
democracy, with unfaltering opposition to those

56

who would render us less free and with gentleness and warm friendship toward his co-workers, Chester Snow has led the campaign efficiently and valiantly.

"With abiding gratitude and affection we tender him this memento of years of treasured association."

The breadth of your service to the community, Chester, has indeed been outstanding. You should have a great sense of satisfaction in the splendid contribution you have made to the advancement of human values. You have effectively assisted in increasing understanding and cooperation among all peoples and groups. Your great abilities have been devoted to a high purpose. You are helping to keep alive in the heart of humanity the bright hope that freedom will some day supplant tyranny and oppression.

INTRODUCING GUEST-OF-HONOR

I now give the audience the real gift of the occasion, Mr. Chester Snow. I have admired his strong sense of obligation to the community and the manner in which he discharges that responsibility. He performs great things for the community without fanfare and in most instances without any particular type of public recognition. I present with considerable pleasure, Mr. Chester Snow.

APPRECIATION AND ACCEPTANCE

I appreciate the attendance here this evening of so many of my friends. The demonstration of your affection is in itself compensation for my years of community service. To all, my heart goes out in thankfulness for your kind words and generous tributes. I thank God for the bounties I have received, for the wonderful friends I have and the fine family that He has given me. Finally, may He give me a wise and understanding heart so that when the final chapter is ended and the Book is closed, history may record my devotion to the cause of the Brotherhood of man under the Fatherhood of God.

I am singularly rich in friendships. Friends of all ages have contributed enormously to my happiness and helped me greatly in times of need. I learned one of the great secrets of friendship early in life—to regard each person with whom one associates as an end in himself, not a means to one's own ends.

Edwin Markham wrote:

"There is destiny that makes us brothers,
None goes by his way alone,
All that we send into the lives of others,
Comes back into our own."

Thank you very, very much for coming here. I deeply appreciate all that has been said.

CLOSING REMARKS

Every now and again a leader arises in the community who attains wide distinction and repute because of his qualities of mind and character. Such a person is Chester Snow— a vigorous champion of justice and equality for all our citizens.

It is my fervent wish that the honor and happiness which Chester and his family are now enjoying may continue and increase for the rest of their days.

I will close by reciting the legend etched on the base of the Statue of Liberty on Bedloe's Island in New York harbor:

"Give me your tired, your poor,
Your huddled masses yearning to breathe free,
The wretched refuse of your teeming shore.
Send these, the homeless, tempest-tossed to me:
I lift my lamp beside the golden door."

N. MENTAL HEALTH FUND DRIVE

OPENING STATEMENT

The Mental Health Fund Drive is under way in our community. We desperately need funds and volunteers. It is my sincere hope that you will open your heart as never before and give generously of your time and money. On all sides we see signs of an awakened interest in the grave problem of mental health. We have become aware that our thrift in research spending has been very costly in human misery. The greatest public health problem today is not heart disease, cancer or any other ailments which have received widespread attention in recent years. The number one health problem is mental illness. Mental illness is among the dreaded afflictions of mankind. Half the hospital beds in the United States are occupied by mental patients.

INTRODUCING PUBLIC OFFICIAL

I present to you a public official who has worked in the interest of the community and is thoroughly familiar with the urgent need to set up an intelligent program for the mentally ill. He has done much in his official capacity as head of the Health Department to intensify research and to provide the sick and needy with the benefits of early treatment which is so vital to them. He is a civic-minded person with a wealth of common-sense and a big heart. Commissioner of Health—Frank Flood.

APPEALING FOR FUNDS AND VOLUNTEERS

It is a privilege and a duty to speak for the Mental Health Fund which cares for the mentally sick of all races.

It is a privilege because in America each of us has the freedom to exercise his own will in the administration of his personal affairs—it is a duty because each of us must be ever mindful of his sacred obligation under the common Fatherhood of God to help care for sick, needy and underprivileged. Freedom to give is one of our great freedoms, and with all my heart, I endorse this appeal for volunteers and funds to establish additional facilities which are needed so desperately. I recommend it to the generosity of men and women of all faiths. Woodrow Wilson said: "The highest form of democracy is the spontaneous cooperation of a free people."

The urgent task of meeting the health and welfare needs of the community cannot be performed by the municipality and the welfare agencies alone. They have neither the funds nor the personnel to meet these needs. It requires the assistance of all citizens of the community. We need private as well as public welfare agencies and programs to take care of our most pressing burden—human need and distress. We cannot afford to have less private welfare. We need more of it. The Mental Health Fund is an investment in the future of America. It represents a duty that has to be met. It is heartbreaking to hear the appeals of persons who need help and to be not able to heed them.

Almost daily we have been forced to turn away from our hospitals many of the sick and afflicted for lack of necessary services. We must add new facilities to keep pace with the growing demands for help. The program of the Mental Health Fund includes enlargement of research, intensification of early treatment, establishment of psychiatric facilities in communities, stimulation of training of professional personnel and the discovery of methods to prevent relapses. It is indeed well to minister to and look after our sick. However, one cannot overlook the extreme importance of doing everything in our power to eliminate the cause and thus reduce the suffering.

The doors of our hospitals should be open to everyone regardless of race, creed or ability to pay. The project needs the support of all who can give and all those who can give only a little can still have the sense of full participation in a great neighborhood undertaking.

Thanking Speaker

Every citizen of the community owes Commissioner Flood a debt for his conscientious performance of the duties of his office and for the many tasks he has voluntarily assumed.

Closing

This appeal for funds and volunteers affords an opportunity for needed community service to contribute to man's ultimate victory over one of its greatest scourges. We have an opportunity to support the continuing campaign for mental health. One cannot overlook the extreme importance of doing everything in our power to eliminate the cause and thus reduce the suffering.

We can combat mental illness by furthering research, training personnel and by providing the mentally ill with hospitals and clinics. It is a community effort we should all assist.

O. HOSPITAL FUND DRIVE AND TESTIMONIAL

OPENING STATEMENT

We have convened today for the purpose of paying homage to Chester Jones who has done so much for Hope Hospital and at the same time direct attention to the financial needs of the Hospital.

It is fitting that our guest-of-honor be singled out for these honors because he has given to the cause of humanity years of unselfish devotion. He is a high-minded, public spirited person. His many philanthropies entitle him to the lasting gratitude of his fellow-citizens.

INTRODUCING DONOR OF AWARD

It is particularly appropriate to have with us tonight a devoted colleague of our guest-of-honor. I present to you the able and industrious chairman of the Board of Directors of Hope Hospital who will make a presentation to Mr. Jones. It is my honor to introduce Mr. Carl Carrol.

PRESENTATION

On behalf of the Board of Directors of Hope Hospital, it is a pleasant privilege to present to you, Chester Jones, this silver plaque. It is inscribed:

"To Chester Jones: In grateful recognition of your distinguished service in behalf of all people, your philanthropies to the community and, most especially, your devotion and achievements in behalf of Hope Hospital. We salute you on the occa-

62

sion of the Testimonial Banquet in your honor tendered by the Board of Directors of Hope Hospital."

The names of the members of the Board appear at the end of the inscription. This presentation reflects a long established custom of presenting silver objects to individuals for outstanding services or deeds. The intrinsic value of this silver plaque is not great. Our concern is that you have some token of our regard and also a reflection in some measure, at least, of all the good work you have done. Please accept this gift as an expression of our sincere gratitude. Your loyalty, your tireless efforts and lasting contributions to Hope Hospital well merit this recognition. It is our fervent hope that you may long enjoy health and happiness. May good fortune always be with you!

Introducing Donor of Gift

Our next speaker is one of the honored gentlemen of this community. He has held many important positions of trust and continues to hold public office. He has given many years of his life to the service of good government and to the honest administration of his office. He is a member of the State legislature. He has come to make a presentation to our guest-of-honor on behalf of Hope Hospital. I take pleasure in presenting Senator Samuel Shield.

Presenting Check

I was very happy to be asked to come to say a few words of greeting to our guest-of-honor. We are all delighted that this gives us an opportunity to pay tribute to you, Chester Jones, in recognition of your activities on behalf of Hope Hospital and your contributions to the welfare and well-being of your fellow citizens. You have the satis-

63

faction of knowing that hundreds of persons have been made healthier and their lives more fruitful because of your activities. We, on the Board of Directors, know first-hand of your deep-seated devotion to Hope Hospital. We have found you a wise and friendly counselor. In spite of the heavy pressure of business matters you always seem to find time for any task, however onerous, that benefits the community.

The dinner committee, consisting of John Jones and Mary Brown, has handed to me a check for $50,000 payable to the order of Hope Hospital, the proceeds of this excellent event, to promote and continue the work of Hope Hospital. It is my privilege to hand this check to you.

May I add that you well deserve the signal recognition you are receiving tonight.

INTRODUCING HOSPITAL OFFICIAL

I now call upon the director of research and laboratories at the Hope Hospital who is performing a great service not only to the Hospital but to the community—Dr. Gilbert Glay.

TRIBUTE TO GUEST-OF-HONOR AND APPEAL FOR FUNDS

It is a privilege to have a part in these ceremonies honoring Chester Jones who has been the guiding force behind the Hospital campaign. I know it may become wearying to listen to enumerations of your services to the community, Chester, so I shall not inflict more on you than the occasion demands. I shall rather emphasize the need for every member of the community to help us raise the money to sustain the work of the Hospital. We need the help of every resident if we are to raise the $100,000 to run and expand our Hospital. There can be no more worthy cause than to see to it that the sick and needy have the necessary facilities for restoring them to health. To help insure a greater Hope Hospital, we are trying to raise the money by public subscription. Many individuals, families, business and professional firms already have contributed liberally to the fund. All who live or work in the area served by the Hospital are being asked to join their fellow-citizens in accepting a share of the responsibility of the project. The movement to enlarge and modernize Hope Hospital now in progress is of the utmost importance to those who live in this community. Additional facilities are vitally needed because of the new housing which is swelling the population.

I am certain that you will have a sense of satisfaction in knowing that you participated in so worthy a cause. Only public contributions support our program of treating patients, carrying forward research and training personnel. It is difficult for a contributor to fully realize how much each dollar means. Please contribute whatever you can afford—your gift in any amount will be gratefully received by the Hospital.

INTRODUCING GUEST-OF-HONOR

The spotlight is unstintingly and unwaveringly on our guest-of-honor. It is difficult for me to add to the plaudits accorded Chester Jones. In view of his successful efforts for so many years on behalf of the community the praise is not out of place. Mr. Jones would be long remembered if he had only half or a quarter of his career on the record. But it is a satisfaction to believe, as well as to hope, that his work is not nearly done. We need his mature mind. We are lucky that we have him. I present the guest-of-honor, Chester Jones.

ACKNOWLEDGING APPRECIATION

This has been a great night for me and it has brought me much joy. The knowledge that what I have been doing for the Hospital and the community is appreciated gladdens me. I had never anticipated tributes as warm as these.

I am very thankful to you. I cannot, however, bring these remarks to a close without publicly expressing my gratitude to the directors of Hope Hospital, the civic leaders and public officials assembled here. It is most encouraging and heartening to win the approval of this distinguished group.

I intend to show my appreciation to you for coming here tonight by bringing these remarks to an end. So, in partial compensation for your sacrifice in attending this celebration, I will say only, Good-night and many, many thanks for all the nice things you have said and the things you are going to do for Hope Hospital. And the good Lord willing, I hope to continue this work as long as my health and strength will permit.

CLOSING

When I think of Chester Jones' interest in the Hospital and all his other humanitarian endeavors I think of these famous lines:

> "Not what we give, but what we share,
> For the gift without the giver is bare;
> Who gives himself and alms feeds three,
> Himself, his hungering neighbor and me."

The Hope Hospital is where Chester Jones' heart is and the welfare of the sick has always been paramount to him as it has been to many here. The continued welfare of its patients dictates more facilities, and I am confident that the generous hearts of the community will make this project their own. Contributions in support of this worthy cause may be sent to the Hospital. It will help heal the sick, safeguard the well. Every contribution will be, indeed, a forward-looking investment in community well-being.

P. HUMAN RIGHTS DAY

OPENING STATEMENT

Because you live in the U.S.A., you have certain rights
protected by law. You can worship as you please, write
and speak freely. No one can break into your home or
drag you off to jail in secret. These are only a few of your
American rights. Few people in the world have such rights.
In many countries, rulers gag and terrorize the people,
silencing all opposition to aggression and war. When this
happens, peace is threatened. For that reason, the United
Nations has adopted a Universal Declaration of Human
Rights.

The work for human rights calls for a combination of
high ideals and an awareness of existing realities. While
celebrating the contribution of the Declaration on Human
Rights, individuals should also accept our common responsibility for all that remains to be done over the years
to bring the standards closer to universal practice. The
Declaration which was adopted in Paris in 1948 is the cul-
mination of centuries of struggle for human freedom. Adop-
tion of the Declaration means recognition of these rights,
not by force of arms on the battlefield, but by means of
reason in a parliament of nations.

INTRODUCING SPEAKER

Our guest speaker has been active in preserivng the
rights to print, teach, speak, assemble, petition and worship. He thinks sharply and distinctly. He has never

shown fear of any person or thing that interferes with free men in the exercise of their prerogatives. It pleases me to present to you, Mr. Jay Judson.

Address

The nations which signed the United Nations Charter at San Francisco specifically stated that the promotion and protection of human rights, formerly vested in nation states, should now also be an international responsibility.

The charter's declaration of conscience won it a place on the revered scroll of events commemorating forward steps in this struggle—Magna Carta in 1215, the Habeas Corpus Act of 1679, the Bill of Rights in 1776, the French Declaration of the Rights of Man in 1789.

The Atlantic Charter of 1941 expressed the hope that a peace would be established which would afford assurance that all men in all the lands might live out their lives in freedom from fear and want. The Washington Conference of 1942, the Moscow Conference of 1943, the Conversations at Dumbarton Oaks in 1944, gave assurances to the still struggling world that the conflict would end with the enthronement of human rights.

The Universal Declaration of Human Rights was adopted by the Third Committee of the General Assembly on December 7, 1948. The thirty articles of the Declaration set forth man's inalienable rights in the civil, political, economic, social and cultural fields; the right to life, liberty and security of person; to freedom from arbitrary arrest; to a fair trial; to privacy; to freedom of movements and residence; to social security to work; to education; to a nationality; to freedom of worship; to freedom of expression and of peaceful assembly; to man's right to take part in the government of his own country; to hold public office; to seek and to be granted asylum; and to own property.

The Assembly proclaimed these rights as "a common standard of achievement for all peoples and all nations."

It is hard to believe that there was a time (and not too long ago historically speaking) when such rights could be withdrawn at the whim of an autocratic ruler. It is hard to realize that there are people today who do not have these rights. It is not easy for members of a free world to comprehend the difficulties of living under a police state, where a word that slips out in an unguarded moment can result in an ominous knock on the door in the dead of night.

Get to know the thirty rights which the United Nations has adopted as the Universal Declartion of Human Rights. It is not a code of law, but a statement of principles. These thirty rights may reshape the world.

THANKING THE SPEAKER

I know of no way to better express one's appreciation of a great exposition of a vital subject, vital not merely to the members of this community, but to the public at large, than doing what you did by your generous applause. I think it manifest that we are greatly indebted to Mr. Judson for his learned and interesting talk.

CLOSING

Nothing that concerns the well-being of our fellow men can be of indifference to us. There is always one race, the human one. We are so much alike. The world we want is a world without prejudices, without selfishness; a world of understanding. We cannot have true peace until we have created a world without fear. The subject of the program is one of vital importance which is becoming more and more impressed upon every thoughtful citizen of this land.

SECTION II

EXAMPLES OF LABOR UNION
CEREMONIES

A. CHARTER PRESENTATION

OPENING BY TEMPORARY CHAIRMAN

We have applied for affiliation with the national organization in our industry and our application has been approved. This is a proud day and it is a privilege to be present on so important an occasion. We require the guidance that affiliation with a recognized national body will give us. We need proper training in trade unionism and methods so that we may have a clear understanding of labor's principles.

Today we will receive from the national body a charter or dispensation permitting us to function as a local union.

INTRODUCING NATIONAL REPRESENTATIVE

I present to you one who has faithfully and devotedly served his union for many years, rising from a modest position through the ranks to the position of Vice-President. He is known throughout the labor movement for his many accomplishments and his unselfish devotion to trade-unionism and to humanity. Brother William Wilson.

PRESENTING THE CHARTER

I am happy to be part of the proceeding which will start you on your way to function as a labor union. That function is to give a better deal to the men and women of America and to satisfy their aspirations to maintain the dignity, the pride and the freedom that rightly belong to all free men.

After a careful investigation of your petition for a charter, your application has been approved. The National secretary has instructed me to form you into a local. It therefore gives me great pleasure to turn over to you the charter permitting you to function as a local union.

In turning over the charter to you, permit me to say that you who have been instrumental in the formation of this local have undertaken an important task. Membership in this great organization of working men and women is a privilege combined with responsibility.

Many problems beset a new local that will tax your officers and members. I am hopeful that by applying your combined talents, energies and ingenuity you will solve these problems. I am sure that the National officers and representatives will give you whatever cooperation lies within their power to advance your commendable purposes. You will find a willingness on the part of the office of the National body to assist you. The assistance is yours for the asking.

You are now a regular local of the National body. Therefore, the future of this local is the responsibility of its members. Be watchful of the character of those who seek admission and, if admitted, give them proper instruction and conduct the business of your local in accordance with the Constitution and by-laws of the National body.

I congratulate you on your enterprise in forming this local. We welcome you and wish you well. It has given me great pleasure to turn over the charter to you. Now, by virtue of the dispensation granted to me, I will proceed to install the officers to the end that they may function as the administrators of a duly instituted local. At the conclusion of the installation ceremonies, I will surrender the gavel to your president who will open the meeting and proceed to business.

B. INDUCTION OF MEMBERS

OPENING

This should be a proud day for you. Your application for membership in Local 234, after due investigation, has been approved.

INTRODUCING INDUCTION OFFICER

I take pleasure in presenting to you an officer of the union who will induct you into membership. He has a profound understanding of labor problems and the respect and admiration of the community. He will, no doubt, tell you about this union's history and the rights and privileges of membership in it. Brother Richard Right.

INDUCTION ADDRESS

We welcome you into membership in Local 234. Local 234 has a wonderful history. Many years ago a handful of members joined together for the purpose of improving conditions in the industry. Great sacrifices were made by them to realize their aims. The rise of the union has often been compared with the rise of our nation. Every American is acquainted with the story of how 13 weak colonies won their freedom from the English kings by organizing themselves into a union of states. And as it was then so it is true with us. These old members, who were weak individually, united to get rid of unbearable conditions. These members laid the foundation of our union. But just as the 13 states— once they won their freedom—grew to 48 powerful states composing the greatest nation on earth, so our little union has grown in membership, in prestige and respect. Our members now have satisfactory economic conditions, vacations with pay, welfare and pension funds, insurance, sick and health benefits.

Before you can become a member, it will be necessary for you to take this pledge:

"I do hereby solemnly and sincerely pledge to perform the duties appertaining to my membership as prescribed by the laws of the International Union and of Local 234."

You are now members of the union and I extend my heartiest congratulations.

CLOSING

This concludes the induction ceremonies. I extend to you my own congratulations. I have every confidence that you will conduct yourself in a manner that will bring credit to you and your union.

You will be presented with a copy of our union constitution. Read it, know it; let it be your guide.

C. INSTALLATION OF OFFICIALS

OPENING

We are here to install our newly elected officers. The officers you elected have wide powers. They have been given the right to decide questions which will effect you, your families, your mode of living, your peace and happiness.

Our union has a wonderful history. A great opportunity lies ahead to continue the high standard of its methods and objectives. You are part of an industry that has been a pillar in the American way of life — by upholding that way of life we can have as glorious a future as is our past.

The decisions of the officers you have elected must be wise and just. Fortunately, the officers you chose have the wisdom and knowledge essential for a successful and just administration.

INSTALLING PRESIDENT

You are possessed of the ability to lead men. The office of president requires a man of knowledge, ability and fortitude, and above all, with a heart and mind imbued with a passion for justice. You have all these qualifications. The membership are fortunate, indeed, that you have been selected to this important position. You have been chosen to lead them, to inspire them and to guide them.

It is my function, as it is my privilege and pleasure, to install you into office. As I hand you the gavel, which is the emblem of your office, it is a great satisfaction to me to welcome you as the new president. You are alert, friendly, ingratiating, well-poised and confident. You are, in every way, worthy of the honor conferred upon you tonight. I

77

know that the leadership which you now assume is in safe and capable hands. The gavel is now yours (*hands over gavel*). With it goes a warm welcome to the new leader and a pledge from every member to work with you toward the high goals of a new year. And now, with my best wishes and with every confidence in your success, I turn over to you the presidency and the captaincy of the organization. I will now administer the oath of office.

"I do hereby solemnly and sincerely pledge my honor, in the presence of the witnesses here assembled, to perform the duties appertaining to my office, as prescribed by the laws of the National to the best of my ability, and to bear true allegiance to this National Union. I do further pledge to deliver to my successor in office all books, papers and other property of the National Union that may be in my possession or under my control at the close of my official term. Further, I do solemnly swear (or affirm) that I am not a member of the Communist Party or any organization which advocates the overthrow of the government of the United States or Canada by force, violence or other subversive or unconstitutional methods, and during my term of office I will not knowingly aid or support the activities of any such party or organization."

Installing Vice-President

Our Constitution provides that the Vice-President is to perform all the duties of the President in his absence and to take the chair whenever he so requests. You have heard me describe the powers and responsibilities of the office of President. Those powers and responsibilities are also yours. (*Administers oath.*)

INSTALLING SECRETARY

The skillful performance of your duties is of the highest importance to the welfare of the union and its members. The qualities which distinguish a good secretary are intelligence, prompt attention to business, integrity in all his dealings with the union and its members. The records you prepare will be the monument by which your work will be remembered. The office of secretary should be given to men of the strictest integrity. But once a union has a true and trusted secretary, it should not dispense with his services but continue to elect him as long as he can be prevailed upon to serve. A union which has secured for this office a man who is as interested in his work as you are will do well to value him highly. (*Administers oath.*)

INSTALLING TREASURER

The treasurer's duties are to receive and be responsible for the safekeeping and to account for the general funds of the union. We know you will garner and prudently manage the funds of the organization. (*Administers oath.*)

INSTALLING EXECUTIVE BOARD

Each of you has been elected by the membership to serve two years on the all-important executive board. The responsibility of the executive board cannot be overstated. The executive board is often the court of last resort. Every member of the executive board should make a determined effort to be just and fair. (*Administers oath.*)

CLOSING

In accepting leadership you, our new officers, have dedicated yourselves to the service of our union. In return, the members pledge to work untiringly at your side in advancing the goals of trade unionism. We know that the great achievements of the past will be the basis for further advances in the future. Under the inspiring leadership of our new officers I know we will continue to thrive and prosper.

D. RETIREMENT OF SECRETARY

GREETING AND WELCOME

We have convened to pay tribute to Arthur Ogden upon his retirement after 25 years of service to our union as secretary. He has well earned retirement from his duties. Much of the executive work, supervision and direction in the past rested upon his shoulders.

It is very fortunate for a union, a cause or a group to find one who is committed to its welfare intelligently, enthusiastically and efficiently as is Arthur. We are happy that this busy, useful life is not being permitted to pass without paying tributes of respect, appreciation and affection. And it is infinitely more important that these tributes be paid while he can yet know, hear and feel them.

INTRODUCING SPEAKER

The man who will represent us in paying homage to one who merits our esteem and affection is not only a colleague of the guest-of-honor, but also occupies a distinguished position in many fields of public work and social service. Throughout his career he has rendered service to the labor movement and the community far beyond the call of duty. His brilliant mind, warm heart, strong character and wise judgment set him apart. It is my pleasure to present Bernard Brooks.

TRIBUTE

The key man in this local is the man we are honoring, our esteemed Arthur Ogden. During installations we are accustomed to hear that the secretary assumes the duties of recording the proceedings. This seems a simple enough task but in practice it really isn't. The discharge of the secretary's duties requires the talent and skill of a diplomat. It would be impossible to detail all his duties. He is the balance wheel charged with the responsibility of seeing that everything keeps on an even keel. He is the first in his place at meetings and the nature of his duties is such that he can scarcely avoid being the last to leave the meeting room. He must accomplish all his duties with tact, with diplomacy and yet with enthusiasm.

Arthur, you are retiring from office but you cannot retire from the place which you hold in our hearts. The committee has a little gift for you. It is a diplomat's bag or attache case. It is our hope that the Almighty God will fill it to overflowing with all the goodness and happiness in life. Good luck to you in retirement — to you and your family, all the happiness in the world. We salute you and thank you for a job well done. We certainly are going to miss you.

INTRODUCING GUEST-OF-HONOR

The retirement of an official who has so loyally and efficiently served his organization for as long a time as has Arthur Ogden is a great loss. We are distressed to lose him but the best wishes of the board and every member go with him in retirement. We are all hopeful that he will have many fine, happy years from here on. I now call upon our guest-of-honor, Arthur Ogden.

FAREWELL ADDRESS

In relinquishing my office it is with the hope that I have done the best I could and that I have had your sympathetic consideration in my weaknesses. The 25 years have been a richly rewarding experience. I am grateful to have had an opportunity to serve you and have deep regrets in giving it up—no matter how compelling are my reasons for so doing. I consider that the position I held in the organization is one of great honor. I hope that my efforts have met with some measure of success.

I want to express my very deep sense of gratitude for the splendid cooperation which you have given me during my tenure of office. Especially, I want you to know that I have always had the benefit of the services of our Executive Board. There has never been a better Executive Board and, I dare say, none so able, cooperative, so sympathetic and so altogether efficient. It has been my privilege to serve with the finest set of officers in the history of the organization.

From the bottom of my heart, I thank you for all that you have so extravagantly said about my accomplishments and each of you for the courtesy you have paid me by coming here and for the splendid gift which I will treasure. The demonstration of your affection for me is in itself compensation for my 25 years of service. I am honored and I am touched. It is good to have lived and worked with you all. Thank you very much.

CLOSING

Because of the conflicting schedules many who would have liked to be here could not come but sent messages which I will read. After the reading of the messages these services will be concluded. (*Messages are read.*)

E. TESTIMONIAL TO OFFICIAL

OPENING

The presence this evening of so many is convincing proof and a warm and friendly demonstration of the high regard in which all of us hold Benjamin Lane. His career has been one of service to his fellow-man. Few persons in public or private life attain such a high degree of integrity, decency and just plain old-fashioned goodness.

INTRODUCING SPEAKER

I present to you a true and devoted representative of labor. He has been president of Local 234 for 20 years and is also responsible for that union's present position as one of the most influential in the country. He has the respect and admiration not only of the members of his own union, but all trade unionists with whom he works. We are grateful for the many years of fruitful service rendered by him to his organization. He is in addition a civic-minded individual and a humanitarian. I present Brother Foster Brown.

TRIBUTE

It is fitting on this occasion that we take note of Benjamin Lane's excellent service to our union for more than 25 years. It is to him that we owe the existence of our organization. He was one of the founders. In his brain was born the idea of establishing an organization of workingmen. To carry out that purpose he gathered around him a group of capable and idealistic workers whose labors culminated in the formation of the union. His interest in it has never wavered. We have a deep appreciation for all that was accomplished through his efforts, for guiding the union to its present position of influence.

I can think of no better inspiration or example in the labor movement than the career of Benjamin Lane. His many civic activities include directorships in Hope Hospital, Home for the Aged and Camp for the Underprivileged. He is a man with a remarkable ability to inspire personal loyalty and affection. He well deserves the tributes of this occasion.

It is a privilege for me to present to him this medal for "Long and honorable service to the members of Local 234, and the people of the community." His vision, warmth and energy and the role he has played in his union entitle him to this recognition.

RESPONDING TO TRIBUTE

The years I served as an officer of Local 234 have proved among my most stimulating experiences. I am very grateful for the good opinion of the members, my associates and my friends. I am happy that I have merited their high esteem.

Twenty-five years ago a group of workers joined forces to better conditions in their industry. I was very happy and honored to be among them.

I shall always recall with a glow of pride and satisfaction that you have honored me in this way. I feel that whatever I accomplished was due in no small measure to the friendships I made. All of these friends guided and helped me. I am exceedingly grateful for the compliments and the medal which was presented to me. It is at such a moment that I humbly give thanks to the Almighty for the blessings that have been accorded me. God bless you, and keep every one.

CLOSING

Our union will continue to move along, increasing in prestige and influence and dedicated to the promotion of a happier, healthier and more peaceful world for all. We are all thankful that we have been blessed with the devoted leadership of the man we honor tonight. Everyone in the industry, worker and employer, wishes him success and satisfaction in all his undertakings. I hope you have enjoyed the salute to a man we admire, Benjamin Lane. Goodnight.

F. UNVEILING PLAQUE

OPENING

We are here to show in an enduring way our appreciation of the life and works of the late Frank Ford, a labor statesman, a man of inflexible integrity, for the many years of service to the community, his union, and his uncommon zeal and devotion to the interests and dignity of mankind. He firmly believed that community services are a vital part of trade unionism. Unions, indeed, are more than instrumentalities for collective bargaining purposes. They are voluntary associations of free men and women designed to meet human needs — outside the place of employment as well as within.

Frank Ford's passing last year was a sad blow to both trade unionism and the community.

INTRODUCING SPEAKER

I have the pleasant duty to present to you, as our speaker, an outstanding citizen of the community who has had a long and distinguished career in the labor movement. He has manifested a deep and profound interest in the betterment of all peoples. He is president of the Craft Union and is giving it first rate leadership. He is charting its activities with great skill, ingenuity and statesmanship. He will make the presentation of a plaque on behalf of Local 10 of which Frank Ford had been president. I present Brother John Jones.

PRESENTING PLAQUE

It is a privilege to be chosen to present this plaque to the Labor Temple on behalf of Local 10. It describes the laudable achievements of the late Frank Ford. It is proper to place this memorial at the portal of this hall where it may be seen and read by all who enter here. It expresses in some small measure the gratitude of the community and the esteem and affection in which he is held by both labor and management. If this plaque serves to keep alive an appreciation of the greatness of Frank Ford and his accomplishments it will, indeed, have been fruitful. It will have well repaid the wisdom and initiative of those who have placed it here. May I read the inscription?

"For his long and honorable devotion to the welfare and service to the community. His creative vision, executive ability and patriotic interest in America brought him many honors. He showed that labor is always ready to help organize the total community for health, welfare and recreation services. Among the fields which benefited from his efforts are: education, replacement of slums by better housing, medical research and mental health. His conspicuous service to his union merits the recognition of its officers and members and this expression of appreciation."

I now on behalf of Local 10 present this tablet to the Labor Temple.

Introducing Program Chairman

Our enterprising and efficient Program Chairman will make the formal acceptance. Brother Frank Fulton.

Acceptance

The late Frank Ford had a place in the hearts of the members of his union and the citizens of the community. His life will ever be an inspiration to us. Through his con-

87

structive efforts the range of union services was broadened and intensified. For many years he was in the vanguard of the struggle against bigotry, intolerance, prejudice and injustice. He had a determination to help abolish inequalities and redress wrongs. He had a tenacious loyalty to the principles of liberalism. He was an indefatigable seeker and lover of peace. He will long be remembered by the community and the labor movement. Those whom he helped and those who will continue to be helped through his efforts and genius will be his lasting monument. On behalf of the Labor Temple, I gratefully accept this plaque as a memorial to our beloved Frank Ford.

CLOSING

It is proper that we give public recognition of the lifetime of service rendered by the late Frank Ford and his contributions to American life. He gave of himself, time and time again, unselfishly and unflinchingly, in the good fight for first class citizenship for all, for help to our aged, for housing for the homeless, for food for the hungry, and for recognition of basic values.

G. UNVEILING PORTRAIT

GREETING AND WELCOME

I extend a very hearty welcome to all of you. We are here for the formal presentation of a portrait of Maxwell Jones painted by the distinguished artist Raymond Ramon. These ceremonies are being sponsored by Craft Union of which Maxwell Jones, who is being honored tonight, is a past president.

I have known Maxwell Jones for more than 20 years. His life has been so rich and so full that no limited time could contain even a bare catalogue of his achievements. I shall refer simply to his deep interest in labor, in people, in worthy causes, in government — national, state and county — his great sense of humor, his enthusiasm, his unflagging zeal, his intelligence, his understanding, and above all his integrity. He has set an example of public service to his community and to all humanity.

INTRODUCING PROGRAM CHAIRMAN

We owe a debt of gratitude to our Program Chairman for his boundless enthusiasm and invaluable assistance in many ways. He has been asked to make the presentation of the portrait of our guest-of-honor. It is a privilege to present, Mr. Richard Morrow.

UNVEILING PORTRAIT

When a man stands heads and shoulders above the crowd there are good reasons for it. As president of the Craft Union, Maxwell Jones brought to that position his rich experience. To the solution of problems of the union he brought a keen and brilliant mind. His energy and drive gave new impetus to the union's leadership. His vision and sound judgment have helped to steer the ship of the organization away from dangerous shoals and on a true course. In his social and communal activities, he has established a rare pattern — a combination of humility and dignity, courtesy and firmness, kindness and devotion to duty.

Maxwell Jones possesses rare qualities of character. He has been a source of inspiration to many of us in the last 10 years. To me, personally, he has been a man's most valued treasure — a loyal friend. I know of no one in the community who is more respected and admired than Max.

In unveiling the portrait of a true gentleman whose career has been so full of inspiration, whose accomplishments are an outstanding credit to him and whose future still lies ahead of him, we perform an act that is and will become even more significant in time to come. Mr. Jones, we are proud to honor you who have brought so much honor to us. We wish you and your family good health and happiness and many, many years in which to enjoy the respect and admiration of your fellow citizens. Now, before I remove the veil from the portrait, I would like to say that there is a brass plate attached to the frame which has the following legend:

> "Maxwell Jones, president of Craft Union: presented by his friends in acknowledgment and appreciation of the true, faithful and outstanding services rendered by him."

I take pleasure in unveiling the portrait and presenting it to the Labor Temple. This is a rare and unusual happening since it marks a gracious expression of appreciation which is usually indulged in only after the completion of a man's activities. This portrait is a symbol of our affection and love for Maxwell Jones.

It was for these reasons that we decided it would be proper that a portrait of Maxwell Jones be prepared to take its place with those of his predecessors in office. The artist has done his work nobly. A good portrait is said to be a kind of biography. You are about to see it and can judge for yourselves.

In the years to come, I hope this portrait will serve as an ever continuing inspiration and that there will be many others whose labor will deserve perpetuation of their features on these walls in recognition of their services. I am sure it will be a satisfaction to all of his friends that the portrait of Maxwell Jones is displayed in a prominent place in the Hall of the Labor Temple.

THANKING PROGRAM CHAIRMAN

If all of the members of the union could know, as some of us do, of the very arduous labors performed by Mr. Richard Morrow during the past year, I know you would share with us real gratitude for his very successful effort. The thanks of the union go to him for the hard, conscientious and fruitful work he has done.

INTRODUCING GUEST-OF-HONOR

It is the duty of the toastmaster to introduce the speakers in brief terms. Although I could say a good deal more about our guest of honor. I will limit myself to presenting him to you as one who contributed to an outstanding degree in making our community a citadel of promise — our guest-of honor, Maxwell Jones.

ACCEPTANCE AND THANKS

I am overwhelmed that I have been thought worthy of so signal an honor. I am deeply touched because this is the first time I have been so honored.

The artist who painted this portrait is to be congratulated on what he has done. He did a marvelous job with a very poor subject. This portrait hangs among my distinguished predecessors as a memorial. If you are to remember me at all, I hope that the recollection will be of one who tried to do the best he could. I assure you that it will always be a matter of great pride to have my portrait in the Hall of the Labor Temple.

I deeply appreciate Brother Morrow's kindness in making the presentation. I am indebted to you, Mr. Chairman, for the excellent way in which you officiated at these impressive ceremonies. Thank you all.

CLOSING

It has been a privilege for me to preside at these ceremonies. It has been a privilege to work in daily contact with the guest-of-honor. No man could have a keener sympathy for his neighbor than Maxwell Jones. No president of the union has faced more of the organization's problems or was better equipped to deal with them.

We fervently hope that it is the will of Providence that he enjoy many fruitful years.

H. POLITICS AND THE MEMBER

OPENING

It is the purpose of this meeting to encourage union members to take an active interest in politics. Election Day is the day when each of us can participate in our government—the day when we are called upon to help make the final decision. When one neglects to vote he hands over the rights of running the government. He weakens the political system which is important to his way of life in a free country. Whatever one's politics may be, and whether or not he thinks his choice among the candidates has a chance of election, it is his duty to vote. We show our pride in our country by exercising our duties as citizens. The very foundation of our country is built on the right to vote, and those who don't exercise that right, don't appreciate the real greatness of America.

INTRODUCING LABOR LEADER

The speaker holds a distinguished place in the labor world. He has given us wisdom and courage, dignity and strength. Through the years of trials and tribulations that have beset the men and women of American labor, he has made a contribution that will not be forgotten. It is my distinct pleasure to present Mr. Murray Charles.

ADDRESS ON PRACTICAL POLITICS

When I am introduced in a way that your chairman has introduced me I feel that I may have difficulty in realizing your expectations.

The coming election is of utmost importance to every

member. The importance of registration and enrollment cannot be too strongly stressed. In order to vote for the public officials who will govern you and enact laws by which you must abide—you must be registered. Many of us fail to register because of laziness, forgetfulness or simple annoyance. Many voters who register fail to enroll. Many are suspicious of letting others know their party preference. Others disdain to enroll because of a misguided notion that they are too good for it—that they are "independents." Independence in voting is a fine thing. But this country's government is built on a two-party system and no one can participate fully in the electoral process without being an enrolled party member. We believe in our two-party system because competition in politics makes for better politics just as competition in business makes for better business. Without good candidates there is no real choice on Election Day. Enrollment does not, of course, curtail "independence." How one votes is a personal matter completely unaffected by whether one happens to belong to one party or the other. You do not surrender your independence when you join a political party. Not to enroll is simply to deprive one's self of some of the privileges of citizenship.

Communities are not likely to enjoy good government unless its citizens demand it—and registering, enrolling and voting are indications of their interest.

Thanking Speaker

In common with you, I have listened with the greatest interest to the speaker, Mr. Murray Charles, whose address is thoughtful, informative and able. I trust his plea will be heeded. We want everybody who is eligible to register and vote in the elections because we want the decision of America, not the decision of the minority.

Closing

It is your duty as a citizen to register and vote. New voters especially should take an interest in the political and civic activities of their country. Only in that way can a firm foundation of informed, public spirited citizens be established to accomplish community improvements. Close ties with political activities also will build better citizens of the future. There is a great need for young leadership in politics.

The lack of interest in politics on the part of women is a source of disappointment. I don't know the reason for that lack of interest but it is there. If only women could appreciate the opportunity that is afforded to them in our political system! Women should be encouraged regardless of political faith to participate in their community on a political level so that we will have the benefit of their participation.

Let us elevate the quality of our political leadership by showing more than a passive interest in our local government. Let our young men and women get into the midst of political life. The type of political leadership we get is merely a reflection of community standards.

You have probably been told many times that in a democracy like ours the people get the kind of government they ask for. If they pay little attention to political affairs, stay away from the polls on election day, try to avoid other obligations of citizenship, and in general devote all their time and energy to their own business, they are asking for corrupt and inefficient government—and they usually get it. On the other hand, if they are actively interested in public affairs, determined to have honest and capable men in office, and are willing to work hard to elect them, they will usually enjoy honest and reasonably efficient government.

I. LABOR DAY OBSERVANCE

OPENING

The labor unions have been asked by the national organizations to lead suitable observances of Labor Day to remind all Americans of their priceless right as citizens. Labor Day is a national holiday dedicated to the wage earners of America. In recent years it has not been given the prominence it deserves as a national holiday by members of organized labor because of the many other attractions that are presented on this day.

The man credited with the idea of setting aside a holiday for this purpose is Peter J. McGuire, the founder of the Carpenters Union, who called for a day to "be established as a general holiday for the laboring classes." His idea bore fruit. The first Labor Day started with a giant parade and ended with a picnic festival to show publicly "the strength and esprit de corps of the trade and labor organizations."

Unfortunately, Labor Day has lost the original quality that made it exclusively the Day of the American worker. It has become a great national holiday marking the end of summer vacations and the beginning of the serious work of the fall and winter. It is a day that now ranks with the greatest of American holidays. But it is a day that should have special meaning to the organized worker.

INTRODUCING SPEAKER

I am honored to present an able, honest and courageous champion of labor whose wise counsel and deep understand-

96

ing of human problems have been invaluable to the labor movement through the years. In the labor movement, where the cause of freedom is treasured, his name is held in admiration and respect. We can never forget his service to our cause nor the statesmanlike quality of his leadership. Mr. Vincent Vinston.

Labor Day Address

Labor Day brings back memories of the days not long ago when the rights of workingmen meant little more than the right to work long hours at brutally low pay in unsanitary and dangerous factories and plants—with illness, old age and unemployment constant threats to be dreaded. In those days the banding together of workingmen to improve their lot was looked upon as a "conspiracy" and was punished by the courts as such. In time, the courts gradually found labor organization and their aim legal and so free of the charge of criminal conspiracies. Yet the road was hard and stormy. There have been great strikes since then in many industries. There have been many labor martyrs.

The influence and prestige of labor has advanced considerably in the last century. Peter McGuire wrote, "There was a time and it was not too many years ago when the trade union and the labor movement of America were too insignificant for president, governors, mayors, city councilmen or public men to consider, much less honor. Trade unions were of no consequence; trade unionists were harmless fanatics." Now neither president, nor governeor, nor mayor, nor city councilmen ignore the trade union movement in America. Indeed, the President of the United States helped dedicate the new headquarters of the merged AFL and CIO organizations in Washington, D. C. Governors and mayors now pay heed to the voice of a united labor movement of more than 16,000,000 members. Few pieces of legislation that involve the social usefulness of the country are ever passed through Congress without organized labor expressing its viewpoint on their value or lack of value. Few candidates for public office take to the platform without taking into consideration the viewpoint of the millions of men and women who have banded together in America's great labor organizations.

Some may feel that Labor Day is not of great importance—that it is just another holiday. I think that we should be made to realize that Labor Day is our holiday— the holiday of the workers. It was created to call attention to the fact that labor is part of the mass of American citizenry and not just another day off or to get away for a picnic. There should be a national demonstration by the members of organized labor to awaken their interest in such an important day.

CLOSING

In these days of automobiles people can and do get away and there are a great many diversions. That is why Labor Day celebrations have been reduced to a minimum. I think we should do all in our power to restore this day as the day of labor. We should try to reestablish the idea of Labor Day as the day of the worker so the community may know who the trade union members are. It should be a day set aside in honor of American workers. It should be an opportunity to tell everyone what contributions labor makes, apart from our trade union activities, to the community life. We should revive interest in this holiday as Labor Day, rather than just another holiday.

We will conclude by singing the national anthem. Please rise. (*National anthem is sung.*)

J. MEMORIAL SERVICES

OPENING

Our Union has set aside this month to honor our departed members. In honoring these members we are carrying on a great tradition. In the inevitable course of events our membership loses each year men whom it esteems and loves. We treasure our remembrance of them and have the consolation of knowing that even after death their memories endure to stimulate the noble traditions of our union.

On this occasion we pause to reflect on the many achievements of our departed brothers. They helped make the glorious history of this Union. Today we are reaping the rewards of their steadfast loyalty to the principles of unionism and the many sacrifices they made. It is up to us who are here today to see that this great organization for which they laid the foundation continues to be worthy of their wonderful achievements.

INTRODUCING CLERGYMAN

Our guest clergyman has given great leadership to the community not only as a churchman but also as a civic leader. He is an enemy of prejudice and a firm supporter of the practices and policies which this organization advocates. He practices what he preaches. He has the interest of the entire community and all its citizens close to his heart. We will be honored by having the benediction given by Reverend Fulton Flood.

BENEDICTION

Infinite and Eternal God, Father of all men, our Guide and our Strength: we bow before Thee in this moment filled with memories that bring us to gratitude for this invested life. May this family of labor be Thy humble servant and so attain to the glory designed for them. Amen!

INTRODUCING PUBLIC OFFICIAL

I take pleasure to present to you one who is dear to the labor movement in this community. He has demonstrated a profound understanding of labor problems and has always fought bigotry with zest, courage and imagination. He has our deep respect and admiration for his is a warm, sincere personality. This is a great community and it deserves a great mayor. Mayor Samuel Smith.

EULOGY

Thank you for allowing me to say some things which, though you have heard them many times before should, I think, be said again and yet again.

It is the purpose of this impressive ceremony to honor the memory of those sterling members of a great union who made the supreme sacrifice in the service of their country and their fellowmen. The men whom we honor today have gone on to walk side by side with other great men of your union. By their devotion to the interests of their fellowmen they carried the banner of the union through a half century of progress to the outstanding position in trade unionism that it holds today.

By virtue of membership in your union today you have working conditions that make it possible to enjoy a more abundant life. You have security. You have an opportunity as free union men to exert a reasonable and powerful influence in your industry. You have all these things because of the progressive and intelligent application of a principle which is the very foundation of democracy—your inalienable privilege of joining hands with your fellow-workers to guarantee a Bill of Rights for labor.

Your union has a wonderful history. Your founders had little to start with except courage and faith in an ideal. When your union was founded working conditions were extremely harsh. After years of sacrifice your union finally attained the purpose of its formation.

It is up to you to see that the achievements of the past shall be the basis for further successes in the future. A great opportunity lies ahead to continue your high standards. You are a part of a vast and expanding industry that has been a pillar in the American way of life—and by upholding that way of life you will have a glorious future.

Roll Call

The officers and members of the Union will rise and stand for a moment out of respect to the memory of our dear, departed brothers whose names will be read by the Secretary. (*Reads roll.*)

Closing Benediction

O Lord, Almighty and Eternal God, Who has domination over all men, may He look down with favor upon the workers of our land. Grant that the decisions of their leaders may always be just because so much depends upon them for the happiness and welfare of our people. Amen!

INDEX

INDEX

(References are to pages)

————o————

A.

B.

C.

105